What I Can Learn From The Incredible and Fantastic Life of Steve Jobs
Published by Moppet Books
Los Angeles, California

ISBN: 978-0-9977145-9-3

Art direction and book design by Melissa Medina
Written by Fredrik Colting and Melissa Medina

Printed in China

www.moppetbookspublishing.com

What I Can Learn From the INCREDIBLE and FANTASTIC Life

─ OF ─

STEVE JOBS

By Fredrik Colting & Melissa Medina
Illustrations By Natsuko Yoneyama

MOPPET BOOKS

Let's get to know Steve Jobs.

He was an American businessman, inventor and product designer. He co-founded Apple, you know, the computer company that makes the iPhone, iPad, iPod, iTunes, iMac and just about everything that starts with an i! He also got Pixar going, the animation studio that has made tons of fun movies, like *Toy Story*, *Cars*, *Finding Nemo*, and *Inside Out*.

Wow, Steve must have been a genius! Well yes, but he also had help from a lot of smart people. People just like you.

Steve Jobs changed the lives of millions of people through his company, Apple. He's been called a GENIUS, MASTERMIND, TECH LEGEND, and the most influential person in the world of computers!

You could almost say that Steve was a

TECHNOLOGY FORTUNE TELLER because

he was so good at predicting what would be the next BIG thing in technology. He was also an incredible entrepreneur, which is someone who is good at starting businesses. *Fortune* magazine even named him the

"GREATEST ENTREPRENEUR OF OUR TIME."

And they don't say that about just anyone!

FUNTASTIC FACTS

ABOUT STEVE JOBS

1 He was adopted when he was just a baby.

2 His favorite college class was not electronics, but calligraphy.

3 He changed his car every six months, but to the exact same model.

4 He thought of the name for Apple Computers after visiting an apple orchard.

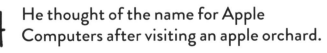

5 He liked to walk around the office barefoot.

6 He once had a famous Japanese designer make him 100 black turtlenecks! That and Levi's jeans were his favorite things to wear.

7 His favorite foods were fish, carrots, and apples of course!

8 From 1997 to 2011, Steve's salary at Apple was only $1! (He already had money and preferred to invest his salary in Apple's future.)

9 Steve owned more of The Walt Disney Company than any single person in the world.

10 He's even got his own holiday! The governor of California declared October 16th to be "Steve Jobs Day."

LET'S START FROM THE VERY BEGINNING...

Steve Jobs was born in San Francisco, California, on February 24, 1955. His birth parents were young and felt they couldn't take care of him, but luckily, Steve was adopted right away by a nice couple named Paul and Clara Jobs who lived in Mountain View, California. Growing up, Steve's favorite thing was working in the garage with his dad.

Going to school, however, was NOT his favorite. Steve was a smart kid and felt that his school was, well...kind of boring. He was also bullied for being a bit of a loner. Seeing that Steve was having a hard time, his parents decided to move to a better school district in a nearby town called Los Altos. After that, his life started to change for the better.

When Steve was 12 he needed some parts for an electronics project he was doing. So he called up the owner of the large computer company, Hewlett Packard, and just asked for them. This was a gutsy move for a 12 year old, but he got the parts and even a summer job at the factory.

While working at Hewlett Packard, he became friends with a guy named Steve Wozniak who was 18 and also into electronics. In fact, "Woz," as he was nicknamed, was a computer whiz. Little did Steve know at the time that the two Steves would later start a computer revolution together!

During high school Steve also became very interested in art, music, and literature. He grew his hair out and decided he didn't really like wearing shoes. His classmates described him as...

"KIND OF A BRAIN

SHAKESPEARE

KING LEAR

ABLO PICASSO

EIINGWAY

KIND OF A HIPPIE"

But he never really fit into either group, which made most people still see him as an outsider.

After graduating from high school, Steve took some classes at Reed College in Oregon. It was a pretty expensive school though and he knew his parents couldn't afford it, so he dropped out. But Steve never stopped learning—even if it wasn't in the "normal" ways.

Then in 1973, he got a job with the video game maker, Atari. It was a good job, but Steve was interested in more than just working and electronics.

He was also curious about the meaning of life and spirituality. So he decided to take a break from work and go to India where he stayed for seven months, meditating and having new experiences.

When Steve came back from India he wasn't sure what he wanted to do. He even thought about becoming a Buddhist monk! But he eventually went back to work for Atari and began hanging out with his friend Wozniak again. Woz had just invented a new computer unlike anything Steve had seen before. Steve was very impressed and said, "Hey, we should sell these!"

So in 1976, in the garage of Steve's Los Altos home, they formed...

THE APPLE COMPUTER COMPANY!

Wozniak was the brains behind the inner electronics, while Steve's eye for design gave Apple computers their unique outer casings.

Steve was also the real visionary and he knew that

THEIR COMPUTERS WERE GOING TO CHANGE PEOPLE'S LIVES.

Steve had a vision for Apple from the very beginning: to make computers "for the people". They made some of the first computers that were not just for businesses or computer nerds, but for EVERYONE! They used new technology like bigger screens and better graphics to make them more user friendly.

Steve believed that what they were doing was important and should be fun, but he was also a pretty tough boss. He wanted his engineers at Apple to think like artists, and nothing less than creating a masterpiece would do!

It wasn't long before Apple grew into a large and very successful company. And in 1983, after only 5 years in business,

Apple Was Named the Fastest Growing Company in History, and Steve Jobs Became Famous.

At only 23 years old, Steve was worth a million dollars, 10 million when he was 24, and over 100 million when he was 25! He was one of the youngest people ever on the list of America's richest people, and that's all money he made himself—his parents were not rich.

In 1984, Steve and his team developed a computer called the Macintosh. Everyone thought it would be a huge success, but before they knew it, other companies started copying the Mac and selling their computers for less money. Steve was disappointed, and by this time Apple had grown into a huge company with other directors who had different ideas for the business.

One day the directors told Steve that he was no longer in charge. So, Steve made the hard decision to leave Apple, the company that he'd started in his own garage. In fact, both Steves left!

Steve knew that wasn't the end for him though.
Not By a Long Shot!

Because he was full of ideas and he didn't let failures keep him down, he soon started a new company called NeXT, which made even more advanced computers. In fact, the World Wide Web was invented on a NeXT computer. And again, Steve had some really cool designs for these computers too, like a black cube casing.

If you are an inventor and businessman like Steve you don't just have to make the same thing over and over. You can create many different things. That's what being creative means!

In 1986, Steve saw the potential in another great company—this time an animation company started by George Lucas (the creator of *Star Wars*). They had invented a new kind of animation using computers. Steve liked this idea, so he bought the company and changed the name to Pixar.

John Lasseter was the head animator at Pixar, and Steve believed that he and John could change the animation world. It took a lot of convincing, but eventually Steve got Disney to fund Pixar's first three movies. They were made entirely on computers, which had never been done before. So once again, Steve was breaking the rules, and making history!

It takes a long time to make an animated movie though. In fact, Steve had to wait until 1995 for Pixar's first full-length movie to come out, called *Toy Story*. It was well worth the wait because it became the most popular movie of the year! Pixar continued to make dozens of hit movies after that, including *Monsters Inc.*, *Finding Nemo*, and *Cars*.

Then in 1997, something really interesting happened. Apple wasn't doing so well at the time, and they needed new ideas. As usual, Steve had plenty of those. So Apple bought NeXT and made Steve head of the company again.

Steve never wanted to do things the same old boring way. He wanted to inspire people, and now that he was leading the Apple team again, he encouraged the whole world to...

THINK DIFFERENT!

Remember how Steve also really loved music? Well, just like how he knew Apple would change the way people used computers, he now wanted to change the way people listened to music. So they invented iTunes and the iPod music players, which started a music-on-the-go phenomenon. People were movin and groovin all over the place! Then in 2007, Steve introduced the iPhone, and as we all know, THAT was probably the biggest technological game changer of all time.

Sadly, in 2011 Steve passed away from cancer. But every time we use an iPhone, an iPad or an Apple computer, Steve Jobs will be remembered as one of the greatest innovators of our time. At home, and surrounded by his loving family, Steve's final words before he left were simply,

"Oh wow. Oh wow. Oh wow."

Steve was always in search of wonder and amazement in life, so it makes sense that he was amazed even in his final moments.

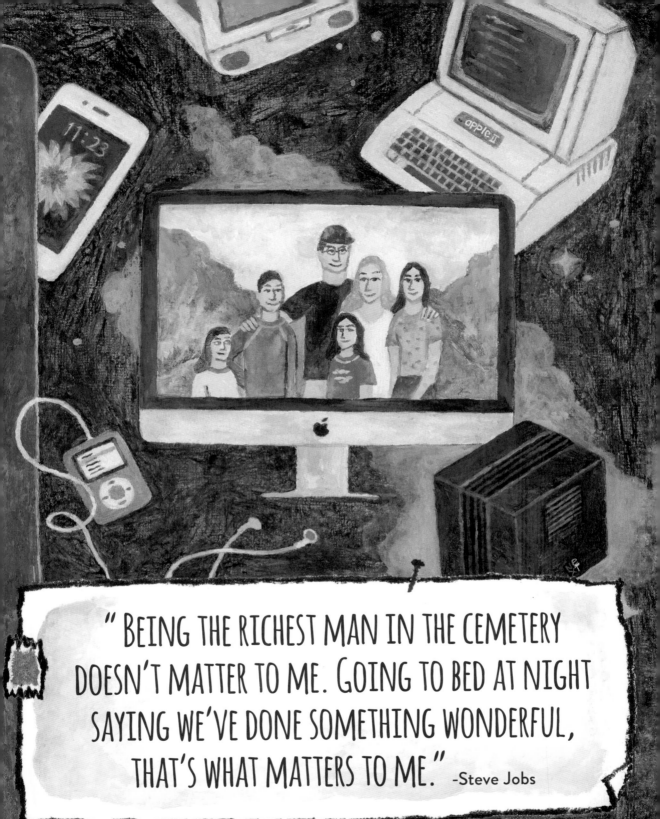

" BEING THE RICHEST MAN IN THE CEMETERY DOESN'T MATTER TO ME. GOING TO BED AT NIGHT SAYING WE'VE DONE SOMETHING WONDERFUL, THAT'S WHAT MATTERS TO ME." -Steve Jobs

The Positively

Let's list some positive things about Steve Jobs and his life.

Steve Connected Us

His vision for Apple Computers gave us technology that makes it easier for people to stay connected and to exchange ideas from all over the world.

Steve Gave Us Great Design

He showed us that everything in the world, even technical stuff like computers, can also have great design. So, it's not just about what something does, but also what it looks like and how that makes you feel.

POSITIVE LIST

Steve Inspired Us

He didn't start companies just to make a lot of money, but to make things that excited people and inspired them to be their best and most creative selves.

Steve Gave Us Confidence

He showed us that there are a million ways to succeed in life, and you don't have to follow what everyone else is doing to get there. Steve liked "the wild ones"–people who weren't afraid to do things differently.

How Can I Be Great Like Steve Jobs?

First of all, you should always be yourself because you are already great! But it is a good idea to learn from people that have experience. Here are a few great things we can learn from Steve.

Never give up !

Things don't always go as planned, and sometimes we can't even do anything about it. But what we can do is choose to never give up, and to keep trying. That's what Steve meant when he said: "I'm convinced that about half of what separates the successful entrepreneurs from the non-successful ones is pure perseverance." So don't give up, just try a new way!

be a dreamer !

Dreamers think about things they want to change or make better. They think outside of the normal box of what's already been done. Some people might not understand your dreams, but don't be discouraged. Remember, Steve was a big dreamer, and he understood that every big idea starts with a dream!

ASK for HELP !!

Steve once said in an interview: "I've never found anyone that didn't want to help me if I asked them for help. Most people never ask, and sometimes that's what separates the people that do things from the people that just dream about them." Being curious, and brave enough to ask, will take you far in life!

BIBLIOGRAPHY

Biography.com, "Steve Jobs Biography.com", www.biography.com/people/steve-jobs-9354805, Accessed February 15, 2017.

Blumenthal, Karen, <u>Steve Jobs: The Man Who Thought Different: A Biography</u>, Square Fish, 2012.

Deutschman, Alan, "Thanks for the Future," *Newsweek*, November 7, 2011.

Grossman, Lev, and Harry McCracken, "An American Genius," *Time Magazine*, October 17, 2011.

Isaacson, Walter, "Steve Jobs, 1955-2011," *Time Magazine*, October 17, 2011.

Isaacson, Walter, <u>Steve Jobs</u>, Simon and Schuster, 2011.

Moritz, Michael, <u>Return to the Little Kingdom: Steve Jobs, the Creation of Apple, and How It Changed the World</u>, The Overlook Press, 2009.

Wikipedia.com, "Steve Jobs", Accessed February 15, 2017.

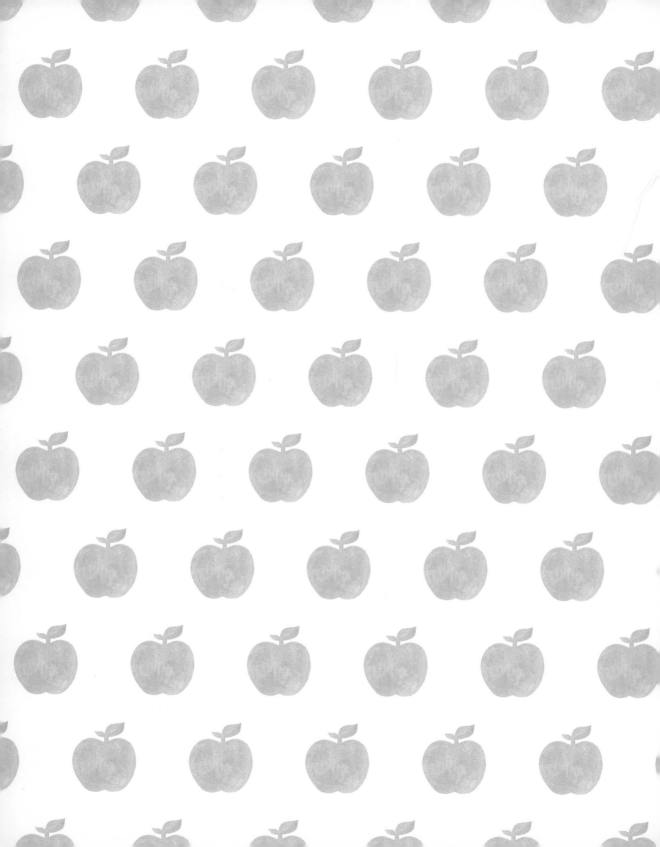